A+
books

TRANSPORTATION IN MY COMMUNITY

CARS

by Cari Meister

PEBBLE
a capstone imprint

Vroom! Vroom!

Cars are amazing machines.

They take us from here to there,
there to here, and everywhere
in between.

Can you run faster than a car?

Today you can't. But the first cars were really slow. They moved about 6 miles (9.7 kilometers) per hour.

People invented new cars.
Some cars did well. Other cars didn't.

How do cars work?
Let's find out.

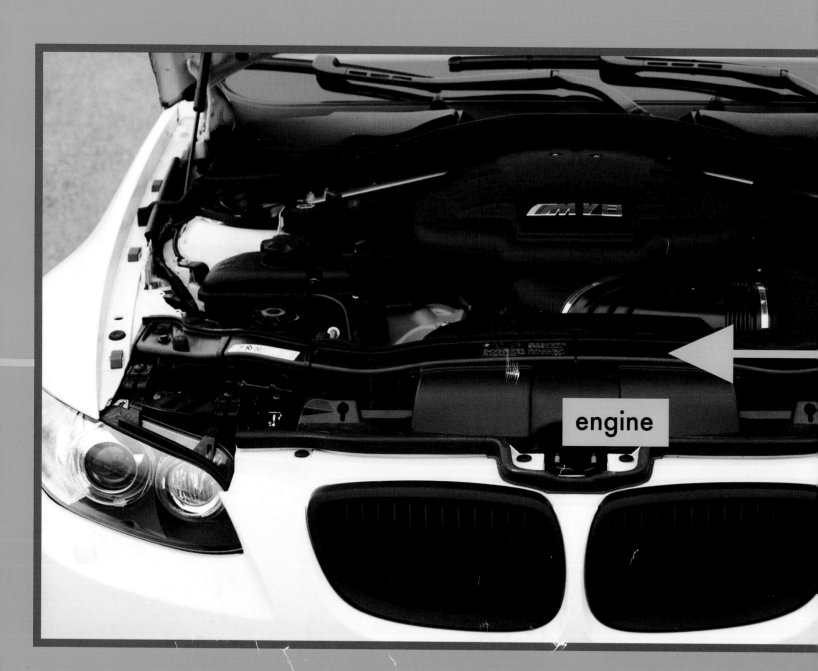

engine

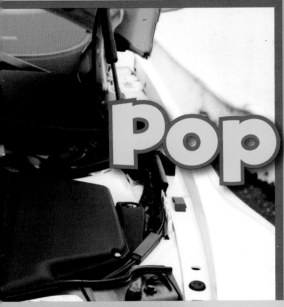

Pop the hood.

Do you see the engine?
The engine is a machine
that makes the car move.

Glug.
Glug.
Glug.

The car needs fuel to get going.
Most cars use gas.
Fill up at the gas station.

An electric car is very quiet.
It runs on electricity. It has a cord.
When the car needs power, you plug it in.

Click!

Ready to go? Buckle up!

ENGINE
START
STOP

Off we go!

To start a car, press a button or turn a key.
The gas pedal moves the car.

A car has a steering wheel.
The steering wheel turns the wheels,
left and right and back again.

Let's roll!

Red light ahead!

SCREEEEEECH!

A car has brakes.
Push the brake pedal with your foot.
The car stops.

The green light means GO!

There are many rules of the road.
You need to learn them all before you can drive.

Pitter, patter.

Here comes the rain.
Turn on the windshield wipers.
Now you can see.

Turn on your headlights too.
They help you follow the road in the dark.

Wee-ooo! Wee-ooo!

A police car is coming.
It has a siren and lights.
Pull over so it can get by.

Zoom! Zoom!

Race cars are fast.
Some can go 200 miles (322 km) per hour!

Someone waves the green flag.

That means GO!

Taxi! Taxi!

You can pay a taxi driver to
take you from place to place.

24

Some people hire limousines.
They are long and sleek.

Pizza, anyone?

Here comes a delivery car with food for you. Someday these cars may drive themselves!

Cars keep us moving.

What type of car will people think of next?

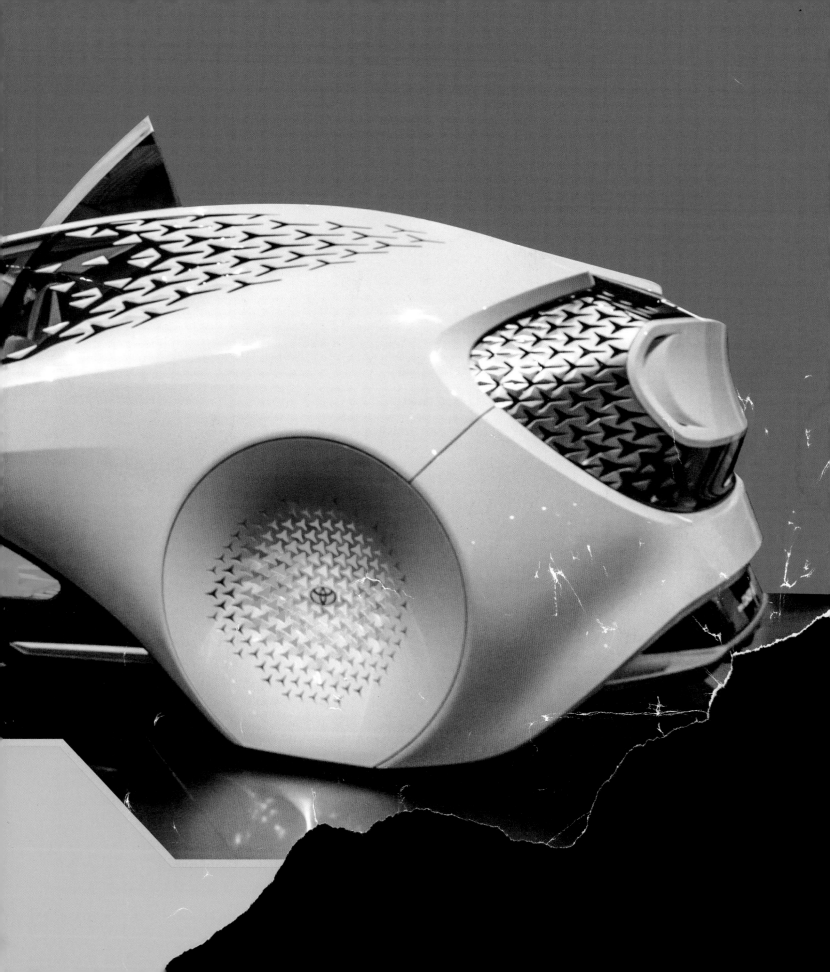

Timeline

1885

The first car to use gas is made.

1903

Windshield wipers are invented.

1908

The Model T car is made. More people can buy cars.

1924

The car radio is introduced.

1959

Seat belts are invented.

1974

The first airbags are put into cars.

1996

2004

Fifteen self-driving, robotic cars race in the first DARPA Grand Challenge near tow, California.

1880
1900
1920
1940
1960
1980
2000

Glossary

engine (EN-juhn)—a machine that makes the power needed to move something

hybrid (HY-brid)—a car that has both an electric motor and an engine that uses gas

limousine (li-MOH-zeen)—a large, comfortable car

siren (SYE-ruhn)—a piece of equipment that makes a loud sound

steering wheel (STIHR-ing WEEL)—the wheel in a car used to move it to the right and left

taxi (TAK-see)—a car with a driver whom you pay to take you where you want to go

windshield (WIND-sheeld)—the glass window on the front of

Read More

de Seve, Karen. *Little Kids First Big Book of Things That Go.* Little Kids First Big Book. Washington, DC: National Geographic Kids, 2017.

Porter, Esther. *Peeking Under the Hood.* What's Beneath. North Mankato, MN: Picture Window Books, 2016.

Spaight, Anne J. *Police Cars on the Go.* Machines That Go. Minneapolis: Lerner Publications, 2016.

Internet Sites

Use FactHound to find Internet sites related to this book.

Visit www.facthound.
Just type in 978197

Index

A+ Books are published by Pebble,
1710 Roe Crest Drive, North Mankato, Minnesota 56003
www.mycapstone.com

Library of Congress Cataloging-in-Publication Data
Library of Congress Cataloging-in-Publication data is available on the Library of Congress website.
ISBN: 978-1-9771-0248-5 (library binding)
ISBN: 978-1-9771-0500-4 (paperback)
ISBN: 978-1-9771-0252-2 (eBook PDF)

Editorial Credits
Parkin, editor; Rachel Tesch, designer;
media researcher; Katy LaVigne, production specialist

Wilkinson, 18-19; ASSOCIATED PRESS: Dee-Ann Durbin, 26-27; Dreamstime: Robert Paetz, 20; Getty
left and top right), David Allio/Icon Sportswire, 22-23, Hill Street Studios, 10, Three Lions /Stringer, 30
creative, cover (bottom right) 2-3, hiphotos35, 12-13, tomeng, 6-7; Shutterstock: Adwo, 21,
ennian, 14, betto Ro top), ameleonsEye, 15, Diego Cervo, 24, egd, 25,
Matti, 28 lio, 11, Nithid Memanee, 8, Photo Spirit,
9